To Hank, so grateful for the tools of the program that allowed us to greet each other in forgiveness and loving kindness during your last month. *-Jane*

To Dad who always demonstrated love and dedicated himself to working a sober program for over 42 years. Forever grateful and I love you and miss you so much! *-Laura*

INTRODUCTION

On a lovely early August evening in 1976 I drank my last alcoholic beverage and watched the sun set over the lake in northern Iowa. I was in turmoil. My husband had driven back to our home in Stillwater, Minnesota in a drunken stupor two days earlier. Just an hour before I took my glass of wine out to the end of the dock, he telephoned to implore me to bring our two young daughters and myself back to our home because he had committed to attending AA meetings. And so our sober journey began. After 40 years of receiving medallions and hearing the question "How did you do it?", I am still flummoxed. My husband and I both had in-patient treatment in Hazelden, supported each other, attended weekly AA meetings and I became pregnant shortly after leaving treatment (causing a natural aversion to alcohol!). I think the answer to successful sobriety lies in the pages of the *Big Book of Alcoholics Anonymous* -- and not for any of my particular efforts. *-Jane*

I am so grateful to be the daughter of recovering alcoholic parents! They instilled in me from a very young age that I too would be an alcoholic if I chose to chemically alter my feelings. I also was aware that the people I chose to be involved with could develop problems if they became addicted to chemicals. I did not know though how my basic sense of self had been affected by the disease, and I did not know how to choose healthy relationships. After successive failed relationships in my young and adult life, I finally entered the 12-step program of Al-Anon at my mother's urging. I was so desperate for relief from the pain and hopelessness that I was feeling that I had no choice but to trust my mom. I forced myself to go to meetings, read the literature, ask someone to be my sponsor, work the steps, but I didn't FEEL any better! I had difficulty understanding the generous guidance. I forced myself to continue! Today, I look back with a smile and extreme gratitude that I knew with all of my being that if the 12-steps have been working for both of my parents for decades then they would work for me too. And they have! *-Laura*

NOTE TO READER

I was in turmoil when my sober journey began. I was reared in the Catholic faith and I absorbed all the resulting beliefs into my cellular DNA, even spending a year in a convent. And I lived my life by those tenets and existed in fear of a God that could damn me to eternal hell for even bad thoughts -- especially sexual. I was arrogant about being a member on the one and true religion and thankful that I had a rigid rulebook for correctness. So how did I end up so despondent, self-loathing, addicted to alcohol and my way of thinking, self-centered, extremely dishonest (especially to myself), always rageful and blaming, compulsive and impulsive, and mostly, terrified of life? It has been a slow and ever-evolving experience for me over the past 4 decades to escape from that personal hell. My profession as a biology, chemistry, and physics teacher to high schoolers; counseling; and most importantly, a study propelled by the 12-step program have given me glimpses of an existing heaven right now. I have studied the Buddha, Rumi, Duns Scotus, the Dalai Lama, Thich Nhat Hahn, Werner Heisenberg, the Quran, Stephen Hawking, and many others to change my perspective 180 degrees.

I think it is beneficial to share my belief system and my particular lens through which I chose my favorite sentences of the Big Book. My concept of "God" is illustrated by iconographer Andrei Rublev in the 15th-century icon named "The Trinity". There are three significant colors in the icon, each illustrating a facet of the Holy One. Gold is "the Father" -- perfection, fullness, wholeness, the ultimate source. Blue is "the Incarnate Christ" -- both sea and sky mirroring one another (The Son is the Perfect Mirror of the Father). In the icon, Christ wears blue and holds up two fingers, telling us he has put spirit and matter, divinity and humanity, together within himself. The blue of creation is undergirded with the red of suffering. Green is "the Spirit" -- the divine photosynthesis that grows everything from within by transforming light into itself -- Grace or the forcefield of Love (The Love between the Father and the Son).

I believe that the Universe began about 14 billion years ago and all of Creation is in the Mind of God and is good and beautiful. The cosmic dance of a few quanta particles and a handful of forces make up an expanding universe of billions of solar systems. This Universe is magical, mysterious, fascinating, complicated and yet ruled by simplicity -- wow -- what a Creator. The Buddhists say that we cannot speak of God because God is beyond human conception. The Jewish tradition tells us that Yahweh (I AM) is God's name. Moses wrote first of this brilliant revelation which alleges that Creation occurred from nothingness. Christians tell us that Jesus (the Son In the Holy One or Trinity) became human and walked on this insignificant planet. Jesus led an ordinary life and because of his radical message disparaging the powers of religion and politics, he was crucified. He showed us how to have faith and love despite great suffering.

I now believe that there are mystics in our midst and I define a mystic as a person who lives in Love and not fear. The mystic is inclusive, merciful, calm, respectful, honest, generous, grateful, trustful, confident, present, and practices faith. Some of my favorite mystics are the Buddha, Prophet Muhammad, Rumi, Gandhi, Martin Luther King, St. John of the Cross, Julian of Norwich, Jesus, Thomas Merton, and Richard Rohr. I believe the Big Book is the guidebook of mysticism in our present world and is the solution to all the addictive behaviors in our 21st century. I feel that I must add a cautionary note and that is oftentimes, I am concerned when I hear superficial or religious concepts about "God, as we understand Him". Perhaps a failure to delve into this uncharted mystery precludes a personal connection to being able to participate fully in surrendering and acceptance to and of life as it plays out each day. So, finally, I believe that we are in Divine Relationship -- to ourselves, others, and all of Creation. We must first learn to love and respect the Divinity within ourselves or we cannot stay away from self-loathing numbing chemicals. And then on to living!!

I believe that we have a "soul" -- a Grace beyond our brain functions of thoughts and feelings. Our mission is to be true to our real self and not a victim of the functions of our animal brains. I believe that we have a mandate to honor, love, and respect ourselves and when we detach from this mission of self care, we deteriorate and experience anguish. The Big Book brings us back from the precipice of self immolation. -*Jane*

"We have found much of heaven and we have been rocketed into a fourth dimension of existence of which we had not even dreamed...The central fact of our lives today is the absolute certainty that our Creator has entered into our hearts and lives in a way which is indeed miraculous. He has commenced to accomplish those things for us which we could never do by ourselves." *The Big Book of Alcoholics Anonymous* p. 25

Enlightenment, resurrection, and rocketed into a 4th dimension all mean to me that each of us is destined to participate in the Divine Relationship/Unity. I actually prefer 4th dimension because it implies a state beyond our three dimensional physicality of space and time. It reminds me that our brains are merely an organ that thinks in the past or the future and experiences resulting emotions. Contemplation can bring me to the NOW and a serenity and peace. I do not know if I have ever been successful but I plan to keep meditating. *-Jane*

What is your concept of the fourth dimension?

"For if an alcoholic failed to perfect and enlarge his spiritual life through work and self-sacrifice for others, he could not survive the certain trials and low spots ahead... Most of us feel we need look no further for Utopia. We have it with us right here and now." *The Big Book of Alcoholics Anonymous* p. 14-15

I cannot believe in a place called hell. We each have Divinity within -- it is our birthright, and I do not think an Infinite Loving God can condemn any creature. But we humans get so easily distracted by things like power or prestige or possessions and our egos "drive our bus". We find ourselves in hell. The only way to heaven is to transform ourselves. I think God speaks to us in the happenings of our ordinary, daily lives and if we accept challenges with faith that all will be ok, we experience heaven right now as a state of being. This is a 24/7 lifetime of making a choice -- live in fear or live in trusting God's love for me. I am bettering the percentages -- on a good day, maybe 50 - 50. *-Jane*

How large is your Worry Quotient?

"The drama of other people's problems can be very distracting, especially when those people are alcoholics. But in Al-Anon we discover that the problem does not lie solely within another person; the problem is also within us. The behavior of an alcoholic friend, spouse, child, sibling, employer, or parent may have led us to Al-Anon, but we soon realize our own thinking has become distorted. Al-Anon helps us stop wasting time trying to change the things over which we have no control and to put our efforts to work where we do have some power -- over our own lives." *How Al-Anon Works for Families & Friends of Alcoholics Ch. 4*

Dear God, H.E.L.P.

Dear God, Thank you.

This is what I do to take control of my life! *-Laura*

How do you plan to take control of your life?

"Alcoholism is a family diesease. This means '...the alcoholism of one member affects the whole family, and all become sick. Why does this happen? Unlike diabetes, alcoholism not only exists inside the body of the alcoholic, but is a *disease of relationships* as well. Many of the symptoms of alcoholism are in the behavior of the alcoholic. The people who are involved with the alcoholic react to his behavior. They try to control it, make up for it, or hide it. They often blame themselves for it and are hurt by it. Eventually they become emotionally disturbed themselves.' (*Alateen---Hope for Children of Alcoholics* p. 6).

In Al-Anon meetings we hear our powerlessness over alcoholism described as: we didn't cause it, can't cure it, and can't control it. We begin to learn the basic Al-Anon premise of taking our focus off of the alcoholic and keeping the focus on ourselves. Hard as it is to look at our own part in our problems, acceptance of Step One brings relief from impossible responsibilities. We were trying to fix a disease---and someone else's disease at that!

To find peace and serenity in our lives, we have to change---a challenging, and perhaps fearful, thought. We may have to re-learn to take care of ourselves. When we are focused on another person's alcoholism and behavior, many of us develop the habit of putting that person's needs first. We may suffer from low self-esteem and not believe that we deserve to take time for ourselves. Whether we judge ourselves as good or bad doesn't matter; we are always defeated by alcoholism. In Al-Anon, we will find help." *Paths to Recovery Al-Anon's Steps, Traditions, and Concepts* p. 8-9

Please help me always focus on myself and how I can offer my best self to the world. I know that I have to be diligent about my own spiritual and emotional sobriety by regularly attending meetings, working the steps with a sponsor, reading Al-Anon-approved literature, contributing to the fellowship and finding my purpose in serving the world. *-Laura*

What holds you back from being diligent about your own spiritual and emotional sobriety?

"We are without defense against the first drink." *The Big Book of Alcoholics Anonymous* p. 24

I think that recovery involves baby steps towards self dignity. Relapse starts with negative thinking about our self-worth and the pain resulting from self-loathing becomes so excruciatingly painful that we believe we deserve to harm ourselves to get momentary relief. Recognizing how fabulous we are as humans and acceptance of our character defects that make us this bewildering species that even God wanted to be part of (the Christian Jesus), perhaps just slowly, we will decide to stay on the path of self care and self love and self respect and decide to feel our real feelings as they come and go. Seriously, when you consider the effects of alcohol and other drugs at your body's cellular level, why would anyone ingest these poisonous substances? *-Jane*

"It is vital to my serenity to separate, in my mind, the sickness of alcoholism from the person who suffers from it. I will dignify him with the respect which is everyone's due. This, in turn, will give him back the self-esteem that is an important element in wanting sobriety. 'The surest plan to make a Man is: *Think him so* (James R. Lowell).'" *One Day At A Time In Al-Anon* p. 264

I intend to treat all people with dignity and love in my thoughts, words, and actions. When I fail, I will promtly admit it and work towards eradicating unloving behaviors. *-Laura*

What can you do to cultivate loving thoughts, words, and actions?

"My old manner of life was by no means a bad one, but I would not exchange its
 best moments for the worst I have now. I would not go back to it even if I could."
The Big Book of Alcoholics Anonymous p. 43

The ludicrous concept that chemically-dependent people are weak willed is an irony to me because
nothing keeps us from obtaining the drug of our choice -- not fears of jail, death, loss of family,
friends, income, or freedom. I had my first panic attack when I was 16 and I was clueless as to what
was happening to me. I quickly discovered that if my parents were unavailable, I became

terribly stressed. This anxiety continued for many years, along with other triggers. Alcohol momentarily relieved my fear of being insane but after the initial calm, I actually ended up with more anxiety as I added alcohol to my body. By the time I hit my critical crisis, I was so self-absorbed, I was neglecting my daughters. I was completely dishonest -- I ignored reality and lived in a fantasy world. Fear drove all my decisions and resentment caused me to blame and scapegoat anyone or thing, except myself. Alcohol and anxiety were a deadly combination for me. Since August, 1976, I began the slow rebuilding of my soul. I have learned to recognize and appreciate all of my feelings. I am no longer in the zone of numbness. I get to be free to experience every moment and that is to be alive, I believe...Yes, I am a grateful recovering alcoholic. *-Jane*

Are you able to recognize the harm you have done to yourself with mind-altering chemicals, in spite of what seemed like a lot of fun times?

"When faced with difficult or painful situations, I can remember that a loving God is always here for me, always available as a source of comfort, guidance, and peace. 'No one is alone if they've come to believe in a Power greater than themselves.'" *Sponsorship--What It's All About* pamphlet

Relinquish control; know thyself; be aware; do the work; trust in a Higher Power; relish the joy!
-Laura

In what ways do you place your trust in a Power greater than yourself?

"Selfishness--self-centeredness! That, we think, is the root of our troubles."
The Big Book of Alcoholics Anonymous p. 62

The Buddhists have a word for this self-importance. Shenpa means attachment to possessions, power, prestige and it manifests in our illusion of separateness. The ego makes the ongoing judge-ments of "I like and don't like". Ego is necessary in the beginning of each human as the sentient baby realizes he is separate from his mother. This separateness continues and sustains the individual for a long time until the big issues of life, death, infinity, suffering, God, and love emerge. Great suffering seems to me to be the best weapon to deflate the ego and the great lie that our egos are in control. Suffering may lead to freedom if we can transform our fearful egos into a soul immersed in the Love Relationship. My daily struggle is to tame my powerful and controlling ego and I need lots of healthy relationships to help keep it in check. Service and gratitude are also helpful for me.
-Jane

What checks can you put on your ego "driving your bus?"

"Resentment is the 'number one' offender." *The Big Book of Alcoholics Anonymous* p. 64

Martin Buber told us that all our relationships bring us ultimately with God, who is the Eternal Thou. For over half of my life, these words were incomprehensible to me. Reared in the Catholic religion, I learned about sin while I was still in a high chair -- most sins were mortal and the punishment was eternal hell where there was fire, gnashing of teeth, devils, and writhing human souls spewing out hatred. God demanded Sunday mass, fasting and abstinence, non-association with any people not Catholic and sex could only happen in marriage for the purpose of making more Catholics. Practice of birth control is also deserving of eternal damnation. To this day, I am unable to physically practice self love. So…I would end up making out with a guy not my husband at a party after having too much to drink, go to confession, and participate in receiving Communion with my family on Sunday. Of course, I professed fear of God's power, said several Hail Marys, and resolved to sin no more so that the priest would grant me absolution. And before I knew it, I was back in the confessional box. Nothing changed in sobriety, except now I made out with a guy from my AA meeting. And so the cycle continued until I fell in love in my early 50s. I had a choice of marrying him or staying an observant Catholic. I could not do both because he did not have a Catholic annulment from a previous marriage. I chose him and then I was truly free. My rigid Catholicism in following doctrines was an obsession of mine.

For the last several years, I have been studying Richard Rohr and I have learned that there were two opposing orthodoxies in the 13th century. The dominant orthodoxy teaches a retributive God and our behavior determines our eternal destiny -- hell seemed the more common ending. The lesser-known orthodoxy states that all of Creation participates in Divine Love and all creatures will be united with God for eternity -- we can be in "heaven" now or, transformation does not happen until after physical death occurs. When I was a practicing Catholic, my ego was in control. I was still dishonest, arrogant, self-absorbed, controlling, fearful, exclusive, and judgemental. But gradually, the 12-step program and meetings and loving people who love me and the words of the Big Book, have allowed me to trust, respect and love myself, others, and God. Now I can trust the "way of Divine Relationship" and am fascinated watching puppies and butterflies, hearing the frogs croaking, being dazzled by light reflecting off water, looking at stars, and seeing the magnificence of a sunset. Freedom from my rigid, righteous thinking has allowed me to accept, respect, and love myself and consequently lose my many resentments -- truly a miracle. -*Jane*

Are you holding on to any resentments?

"We were now at Step Three. Many of us said to our Maker, *as we understood Him:* 'God, I offer myself to Thee-to build with me and to do with me as Thou wilt. Relieve me of the bondage of self, that I may better do Thy will. Take away my difficulties, that victory over them may bear witness to those I would help of Thy Power, Thy Love, and Thy Way of life. May I do Thy will always!'" *The Big Book of Alcoholics Anonymous* p. 63

The Hindu word for people greeting each other with a slight bow at the waist is NAMASTE. It means: " I bow to the Divine in you." Real Love is anything but sentimental. It is the most creative form of human presence. Love is the threshold where divine and human presence flow into each other. All presence depends on consciousness. Where human consciousness is dulled, distant, and blind, presence grows faint and vanishes. Albert Einstein often said that no problem can be solved by the same consciousness that caused the problem in the first place. Thomas Merton wrote that life is our destiny whether we want it or not. If a man wills to remain in what is not, he will hate life and experience the "resurrection of judgement". A Buddhist teacher said to his students: "If I gave you beer and a deck of cards, you will stay up for hours with enthusiasm and energy. But if I ask you to meditate for even an hour in the evening, you will fall asleep." Our egos lead us astray naturally to what provides pleasure. Addiction to a mood-altering chemical as a quick fix to numb any suffering is lethal. Self-reliance always fails. Our egos resist participating in Love -- of ourselves, all others, and God. But if we reside in Love, we become armed with a clear mind, and we will be conscious and present and engaged in the world. We will have the power of Faith. *-Jane*

Is it really our ego that is cunning, baffling, and powerful? Am I letting go of my ego and letting faith/acceptance/compassion/service guide my behavior?

"When we turn our will and our lives over to the care of a Higher Power, we affirm that we need guidance. Our job now is to keep our minds open, knowing that life-changing help can take any avenue, any form, any voice. Our teachers are all around us. Let's make room for every single one." *How Al-Anon Works for Families & Friends of Alcoholics Ch. 9 "Think"*

I pray for daily humility. I pray for surrender to the care of a Higher Power. I pray for vigilance in always having loving thoughts, words, and actions. *-Laura*

How do you turn your will and life over to the care of a Higher Power?

"I deserve to make choices that let me feel good about myself. It may take a while to see results, but I am building a life that promotes my health and self-esteem. It's worth the wait."
Courage to Change p. 342

Rebuild. Repeat. Rejoice.

Having both parents with the disease of alcoholism, I have learned from the womb that my needs come second. This psychological consequence of the disease hindered a healthy formation of self-esteem. After repeated relationship failures, I finally found guidance to build my self-esteem through counseling, the 12-step program and studying spirituality. -*Laura*

What choices do you make that help or hinder your self-esteem?

"Courtesy is an expression of love, warm concern for the other person's comfort, peace of mind and well-being...The practice of courtesy in the home gives us many opportunities each day to convey our love in little ways...I will take every opportunity to be courteous to those nearest me, as well as those outside my orbit. The warmth and kindness of courtesy will take the sting out of resentments, and give dignity and importance to the members of my household, making them feel secure and loved. 'Courtesy makes a less troublesome game of life. Misuderstandings melt away; it gets rid of the avoidable obstructions.'" *One Day at a Time in Al-Anon* p. 159

Getting outside of myself is the ultimate success of joyous living. Living with addicts without the guidance of Al-Anon kept me scared and defensive. Now I work towards cultivating kindness and courtesy, because that is the kind of person I want to be and the life I want to live. *-Laura*

What does dignity look like to you? How do you want to represent yourself in day-to-day interactions? In times of stress? In times of anger?

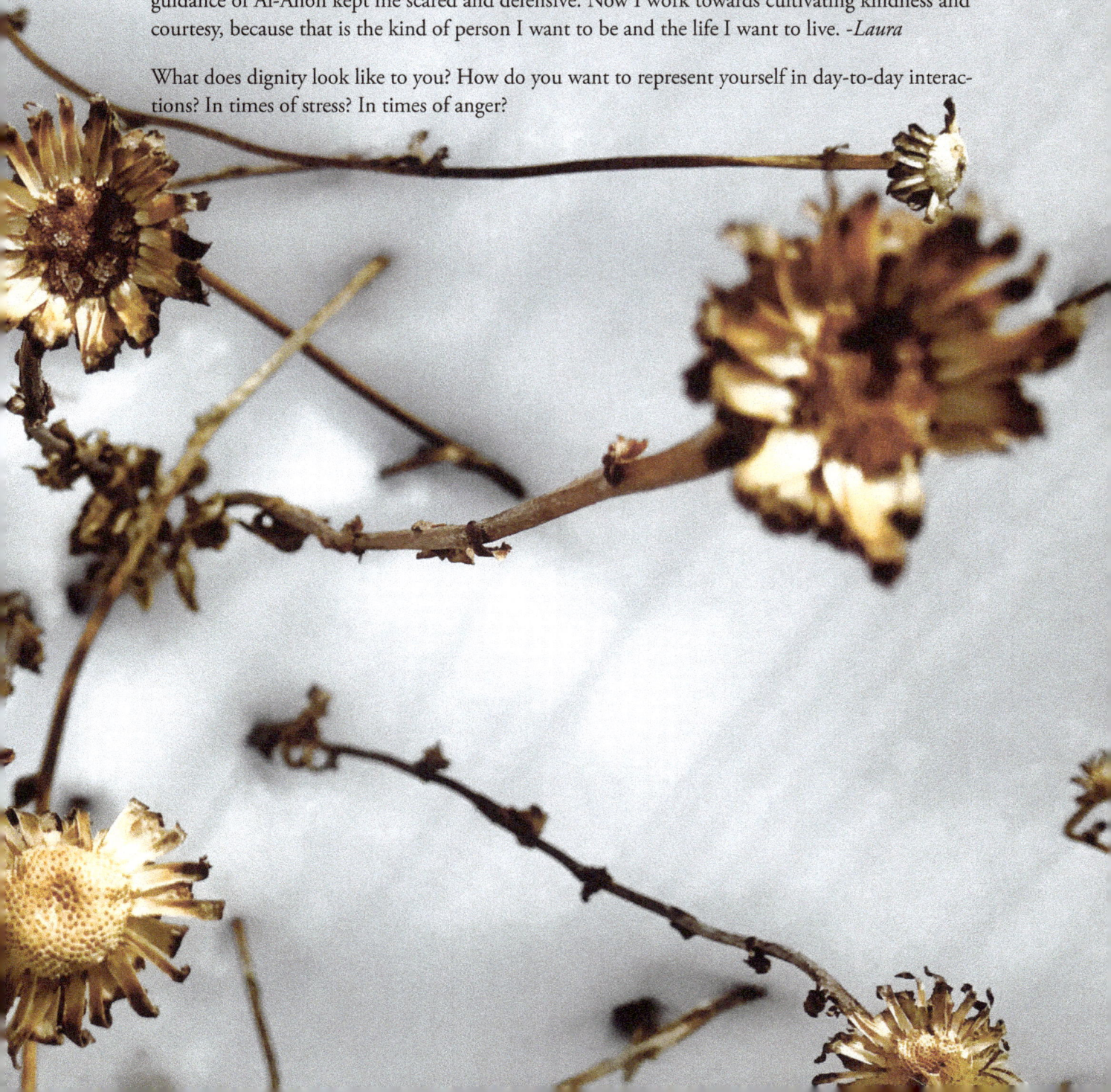

"Remember that we deal with alcohol--cunning, baffling, powerful! Without help it is too much for us. But there is One who has all power--that One is God. May you find Him now!...We claim spiritual progress rather than spiritual perfection." *The Big Book of Alcoholics Anonymous* p. 58-60

The Buddha said: "Like a caring mother holding and guarding the life of her only child, so with a boundless heart hold yourself and all beings." And Walt Whitman wrote: "I am larger and better than I thought. I did not think I held so much goodness." Thich Nhat Hahn states: "Because we are interconnected, when we awaken love in ourselves and express it, our love changes the world around us." Thomas Merton says, "Life is this simple. We are living in a world that is absolutely transparent and the divine is shining through it all the time. Every being becomes the Beloved. If only humans could see themselves as they really are, there would be no more need for war, for hatred, for greed, for cruelty. I suppose the big problem would be that we would fall down and worship each other." The Buddhists believe that the path as a bodhisattva is to not be consumed by blaming and turning on ourselves or others, and to act only out of loving kindness -- to be free to cultivate our talents and to contribute them to the world in service. James Joyce said that mistakes can be "the portals of discovery". So remembering that we are fundamentally good, when we do something intentional that hurts someone, if we can be open and honest and true about the mistake and not allow guilt or shame to overwhelm us, we can learn. We learn to stay present and feel the full extent of what it feels like to have messed up, to have done something that really harms somebody. "Instead of failure and regret being the seed of self-loathing, it can become the seed of compassion and empathy", according to the Dalai Lama. To be human is to make mistakes. *-Jane*

How do you live with your mistakes? Do you still use the word "sin"?

"If I am suffering from bitterness against the alcoholic, I will cling to the thought that my growth and serenity depend on overcoming my animosity. Unless I free myself from it, I may carry it over into my relations with other people, even those who, in Al-Anon, are trying to help me. 'It is not men's acts which disturb us--- but our reaction to them. Take these away, and anger goes. No wrong act of another can bring shame on you' (Marcus Aurelius)." *One Day At A Time In Al-Anon* p. 320

Yes, yes, yes! But this is not always easy to do. I often find myself clinging to knowing I have to overcome animosity for my own healthy living. I encourage myself to keep going and to always try my best. Then in desperation, I remember to turn it over to my higher power! Or to simply ask for help. -*Laura*

What do you do when you find yourself reacting to another person?

"To us, the Realm of Spirit is broad, roomy, all inclusive; never exclusive or forbidding to those who earnestly seek." *The Big Book of Alcoholics Anonymous* p. 46

Richard Rohr tells us: "If you don't believe that infinite Love is the center of the universe, you live in a scarcity model where there's never enough food, money, security, health care, mercy -- to go around. You live in fear and cannot risk letting go. If you are protecting yourself, if you are securing your own image and likeness, then you are holding on. Your ego remains full of itself. I believe institutions and systems are created by the egoic mind and mirror our individual fear-based lives." Ego desires prestige, power, and possessions. Exclusivity, blaming (scapegoating), judging, dishonesty, hatred, lust, greed, self-absorption are presented in fear-based living. But if we choose to let go of our ego and trust in Loving Relationship, we enter into a heavenly and happy existence and a trust-filled life. I think that we can have fear or faith (Love) but not both. I have daily triggers for fear and have to be present to that thought and emotion and know to allow the fear to dissipate and that I will not become its victim. My most grateful recovery gift is to have become a participant in the Realm of the Spirit which means to honor my goodness and the goodness of all others. I now have a life of peace, laughter, awareness, presence, joy, and love. *-Jane*

Can you compare your life before and after recovery?

"Today I have a chance to make a contribution to my sense of well-being. I can take some small action that will strengthen a relationship, pursue a goal, or help me to feel better about myself. I don't expect to dramatically alter my life. My goal is simply to move in a positive direction, knowing that major strides often begin with very small steps." *Courage to Change* p. 38

With the help of Al-Anon, I now know that my quality of life is my responsibility. With specific instructions like these from readings, I have learned how to cultivate my own well-being and self-esteem. *-Laura*

What small actions are you taking to help cultivate the life that you want and the person you want to be?

"...if you wish, you can join us on the Broad Highway. With this attitude you cannot fail." *The Big Book of Alcoholics Anonymous* p. 55

I believe that if we are living lives of Faith in the Divine Relationship and not egoic lives of fear, we are delightfully present and aware of amazing happenings, synchronicities, "God Events", and coincidences. When I divorced my second husband because he relapsed and became abusive, I was devastated. Soon afterwards, I went to Al-Anon and met an amazing guy and we married. He was truly a mystic. When he was diagnosed with a fatal cancer, he lived the next three months completely trusting his God. When I queried him about how it felt to be dying, he answered: "It feels like being in a bus depot, waiting for the bus to come." He died peacefully a few hours later. Now at age 73, I realize that my tough times have transformed me so that I have access to the tools that overcome extreme self-absorption and fear and dishonesty and resentment. Of course, it is not "shangri la" all the time but it is delightful to notice Grace/Love happening daily in my life.

I often say: "It was a God thing!" I had two "Coincidences" early this morning as I began thinking about this particular Big Book quote. The Dalai Lama shared on Twitter, May 13, 2019 these words: "Honest concern for others is the key factor in improving our day-to-day lives. When you are warm-hearted, there is no room for anger, jealousy, or insecurity. Healthy happy families and a healthy peaceful nation are dependent on warm-heartedness." And then I read Thomas Merton's words: "God makes us ask ourselves questions most often when He intends to resolve them. He gives us needs that He alone can satisfy and awakens capacities that He means to fulfill. Any perplexity is liable to be a spiritual gestation, leading to a new birth and a mystical regeneration." As our fear transforms to faith when our egos are shattered by great suffering, we experience a personal resurrection from our personal hell to our personal heaven. *-Jane*

And are you ready to transform yourself and join all your fellow mystics on the Broad Highway of the Divine Relationship? Or do you prefer a different name for the Broad Highway?

"Our goal is to build healthy, respectful relationships. By applying the Al-Anon slogan, 'Let It Begin with Me,' we can see that it is not good enough to wait for others to treat us well before we are considerate of them. Most of us find that after a while we begin to attract what we give out. If we are consistently warm and respectful, we tend to attract respect and warmth from others. It may not take the form we expect or come from everyone we encounter, but if we focus on ourselves, choose behavior we feel is appropriate, and let go of the results, our communication as a whole is bound to improve." *How Al-Anon Works for Families & Friends of Alcoholics* p. 98

It works if I work it! If I can recognize in a stressful situation that I am triggered by another person and pause...usually I can realize that my ego is involved and I am somehow fighting unnecessarily for my self-worth. After practicing the steps of Al-Anon and going to meetings and participating in the fellowship and reading the daily readings, slowly I am saving myself from the destruction of negative thoughts! I now know that my self-worth is always there in the form of my Higher Power, and the more I can remember this the more compassion I exude in all of my interactions. *-Laura*

What helps you to care for your self-worth?

"'When my thoughts are centered on learning to live, I will be less tempted to involve my mind with the thoughts of how others live.'" *One Day at a Time in Al-Anon* p. 215

How I live. How I live. How I live. How I live. How I live...

I constantly think about how others live! I've become aware of when I do it, and I try to trace the thought backwards to better understand my motivation. I almost always find myself trying to stay safe. This can be a distracting and selfish thought that impedes deep relationships. If the thoughts are fearful and obsessive, I know this ingrained habit is taking me down rather than a useful tool for survival. How will this person's behavior/life affect my well-being? This can be beneficial in assessing situations for emotional and spiritual health; however, if it becomes a fearful obsession then it will destroy my serenity. *-Laura*

How many of your thoughts are centered on learning to live? How many on how others live?

"...faith did for us what we could not do for ourselves." *The Big Book of Alcoholics Anonymous* p. 70-71

Google defines mystic: Mystic is a person who seeks by contemplation and self-surrender, to obtain unity with or absorption into the Deity or Absolute, or who believes in the spiritual apprehension of truths that are beyond the intellect. The second definition of faith as defined also by Google: strong belief in God or in the doctrines of religion based on spiritual apprehension rather than proof. My good friend and poet, Barry MacDonald wrote: "There is a deeper part of me founded On a quiet discerning watchfulness. There is a wellspring of essential enthusiasm directing." Richard Rohr warns: "I think this is very hard for western individuals to comprehend. We like to assert our separateness and our specialness, which is the low-level preoccupation of the ego. Only the soul understands itself as radical relatedness. It knows that we are all good with one another's goodness." Thomas Merton wrote: "Love for all, hatred of none, is the fruit and manifestation of love for God -- peace and satisfaction. Forgetfulness of worldly pleasure, selfishness, and so on, in the love of God, channeling all passion and emotion into the love of God." Pema Chodrun, a Buddhist nun also warns: "We live in a painful, self-centered prison called 'me'". The Dalai Lama often quotes the following verse of the Indian sage Shantideva: "All the joy the world contains Has come through wishing happiness for others. All the misery of the world contains Has come through wanting pleasure for oneself." For those of us caught in chemical addiction, we have an additional fear -- a life of misery for ourselves and our loved ones -- prison, early death, or insanity. Our egos are necessarily shattered when the chemicals quit working to help us to feel momentarily better. Brought to our knees, we give up and beg for help. We become fertile ground for the seeds of faith. Most humans are not forced to accept faith. We addicts have to make the choice to accept faith or face disaster. Perhaps we are actually the lucky ones to have our egos forced to surrender in order to live. When I am contemplating what behavior is the next right one, the "litmus test" is the question I ask myself: "Is my ego involved in this action?" *-Jane*

What is your faith doing for you that you could not do for yourself?

"When ready, we say something like this: 'My Creator, I am now willing that you should have all of me, good and bad. I pray that you now remove from me every single defect of character which stands in the way of my usefulness to you and my fellows. Grant me strength, as I go out from here, to do your bidding. Amen.' We have then completed *Step Seven*." *The Big Book of Alcoholics Anonymous* p. 76

My therapist gave me a card that reads: "I love myself exactly as I am. I no longer wait to be perfect in order to love myself." Richard Rohr writes that he hopes humans will get a sense of how the universe is radiant and exciting. The Self-creating universe is indeed God dancing! -- outside Godself, still doing the being, Community, sharing being, indwelling, rejoicing, and alway being more." Barry MacDonald also writes this insightful poem: " I don't begrudge the critical voice its Imposing place within my awareness Because I need a check on selfishness And a sense of justice and decency. But It's easy to belittle myself And to disparage the things I have done And nothing is more destructive of my Peace than persistently negative thought And the daily tenor of my thinking Has the capacity to destroy my Chances for happiness if I give my Punishing monologue too much power But I don't believe I'm alone in thought In the quiet the divine emerges. Without circumspection, gentleness, patience, love, I'm lost." Pema Chödrön reminds us: "Loving ourselves provides the foundation for cherishing others. If we feed our low self-esteem, we won't have anything to build on." Jalaludin Rumi lived in the 13th century and his poetry has greatly influenced the Islamic world since then. Two of my favorites are: "If you put your heart against the earth with me, in serving every creature, our Beloved will enter you from our sacred realm and we will be, we will be so happy." and "A good gauge of spiritual health is to write down the three things you most want. If they in any way differ, you are in trouble."

I believe that all humans have a strong negative voice and we addicts have fed our addictions through persistent self-loathing beliefs and subsequent despair. Only the elimination of our egos and emergence of our Real self (soul) can lead to recovery. And the tiniest of tiny baby steps in the beginning are needed. And I believe that Faith in a Divine Relationship is our only hope. Every day my shortcomings barge through in my behaviors. I am almost always late to meetings. I defiantly break certains laws -- I drive too fast and I do not leash my dog in state parks. I am impatient. I run the leaf blower daily because my driveway must be cleared of tree debris. I worry about getting older. If I look deeply enough I admit that all these defects of character are rooted in fear. Every day I do battle with my ego wanting to "drive my bus" and every day I get to decide to live in faith/love that I will be okay no matter what happens.

Every mystic reminds us that we are basically good and share in Divinity. When we are aware of our shared humanity, we lose our self-absorption and become compassionate towards all of creation. Several decades ago I taught environmental issues to students: population increase, global climate change, species depletion, and poisoning our water and soil. We are defacing this lovely planet and endangering our species. I want to lessen my greed and decrease my compulsion to have a perfect environment in my home and yard -- not consume and discard, minimize my living space, drive less, and not use Roundup or Pine-Sol. *-Jane*

When you look at your shortcomings, can you discern if each one has a fear foundation?

"I try to imagine that my words and actions are being addressed to myself, because in the long run I generally get back what I give out. If I am unhappy with what I receive, I might try looking for that same behavior in myself. It may not take exactly the same form, but I find that whatever I dislike in another is something that I dislike in myself. The reverse is also true: What I admire in others probably reflects an admirable quality within me. There is someting for me to learn from every interaction I have with other people. I will make an extra effort today to take note of the attitudes I'm giving and receiving because they both can teach me about myself. 'Though we travel the world over to find the beautiful, we must carry it with us or we find it not (Ralph Waldo Emerson).'"
Courage to Change p. 302

After practicing this tenet, I am getting faster at recognizing when I get triggered (upset, angry, judgmental, critical, obsessive, defensive, scared). Now when I notice negative thoughts arising, I look within and usually find fear and/or self-doubt. Discovering unattractive qualities within me always makes me uncomfortable; I can feel my face redden and my heart race. But then I remind myself of my humanness and laugh at my stubborn self-will trying to deny my imperfections. Thank God in Heaven for Al-Anon teaching me to let go of my dominating self-absorbtion, denial and self-righteous perfection-seeking. And please forgive me when I still do this! *-Laura*

Who or which behavior makes you really angry? How are you similar?

"Genuine, healthy love isn't self-destructive. It doesn't diminish us or strip us of our identitites, nor does it in any way diminish those we love. Love is nourishing; it allows each of us to be more fully ourselves." *How Al-Anon Works for Families & Friends of Alcoholics* p. 83

When I expected my love interests to give to me the way I was giving to them, I was always distraught and disappointed. Why was I expecting someone to be able to love the way I could love? Especially people suffering from an untreated emotional and physical addiction. *-Laura*

What do you expect from a loved one or partner?

"If we are painstaking about this phase of our development, we will be amazed before we are half way through. We are going to know a new freedom and a new happiness. We will not regret the past nor wish to shut the door on it. We will comprehend the word serenity and we will know peace. No matter how far down the scale we have gone, we will see how our experience can benefit others. That feeling of uselessness and self-pity will disappear. We will lose interest in selfish things and gain interest in our fellows. Self-seeking will slip away. Our whole attitude and outlook upon life will change. Fear of people and of economic insecurity will leave us. We will intuitively know how to handle situations which used to baffle us. We will suddenly realize that God is doing for us what we could not do for ourselves.

Are these extravagant promises? We think not. They are being fulfilled among us -- sometimes quickly, sometimes slowly. They will always materialize if we work for them." *The Big Book of Alcoholics Anonymous* p. 83-84

Christians have the Way of the Cross that leads to Resurrection/Heaven and the Buddhists have the Way of the Bodhisattva that leads to Nirvana. Addicts have the 12-step program that leads to Recovery. I believe that all humans have addictive thinking, and as a result there are no essential differences to any road or Way that leads to transformation from egoic-based fear to soul-based faith.

This is a shortened version of my story. I grew up in Iowa at the end of World War II to extremely exhausted parents. I had two older brothers, nieces and nephews and an ill grandmother living with us. Dad sold life insurance and Mom was a legal secretary. I did not have the feminine gene and grew up racing sailboats, horseback riding, sledding, ice skating, hiking, playing touch football, basketball, fishing, climbing cliffs and doing just about anything to be outside. Needless to say I felt like a disappointment to my family. I got chunky when I hit adolescence and did not date -- until Hank, in my last year of college. We married and moved to Stillwater, Minnesota. Hank taught band until he got home and then he drank -- a lot. And when I was not pregnant with our two daughters and nursing the second child, I drank -- a lot. And we fought a lot. We did all the normal crazy behaviors of an alcoholic family until a crisis occurred. And thanks to St. Mary's outpatient treatment that led to both of us receiving inpatient treatment at Hazelden, we have remained sober. Hank died in 2018. He described me as "a grandiose bitch" in a questionnaire that he filled out for my Hazelden counselor. I was clueless to feeling anything but abject terror and extreme guilt and shame for my unmanageable life and inadequacies as a wife and mother and daughter and sister and teacher. I had no friends.

I think doing these steps for forty plus years and learning things profoundly each time have transformed me slowly, I hope. Each step requires acceptance and trust in others and complete honesty and a willingness to open "the Pandora's Box" of seeing how our mistakes have hurt ourselves and others. Our letting go of egoic fear and making amends allow transformation "half way through the 9th step." One of my first realizations at Hazelden was that this is a lifetime daily practice. Trust me. I have had long periods of "dry drunks" and I think that it was not until the death of my third husband after 20 years of not using, that I finally started to understand and "walk the talk". I discovered a tribe of women who accepted me and loved me and trusted me so that I could finally do so to myself. Al-Anon has enriched my life immeasurably. And the beauty of this program is that it never ceases to amaze me that I can have such joy each and every day if I keep my ego/fears in check. -*Jane*

Are the promises coming true for you?

"What we really have is a daily reprieve contingent on the maintenance of our spiritual condition." *The Big Book of Alcoholics Anonymous* p. 85

In the words of Eckhart Tolle: "Rocks, plants, and animals still know…how to be -- to be still, to be ourselves, to be where life is: here and now." Tukaram lived in the 17th century and was a low caste Hindu, and he wrote 8,000 short poems. He had no formal education. His poetry is exquisite. "I could not lie anymore so I started to call my dog "God." First he looked confused, then he started smiling, then he even danced. I kept at it: now he doesn't even bite. I am wondering if this might work on people." and this one is really the words of a mystic: "so tell me again dear One so clear: I am you."

I think we can participate either in the Divine Relationship or in the addictive relationship to our ego. Pema Chödrön reminds us that the cause of our misery is our neurotic self-absorption. Rather than blaming others for our unhappiness or blaming ourselves in a harsh, mean-spirited way, we need to take a clear, compassionate look at how self-centeredness ruins our chances of lasting happiness. Our relentless self-importance causes us to suffer far more than any other culprit. The Buddhist teacher, Shantideva encourages us to acknowledge the misery caused by our ego trips, and to use our innate wisdom to turn that around and promote confidence in our basic goodness. Life is too short to stay addicted to ego!!! He goes on to urge us to be of service and to smile and to please stay awake. The bodhisattva delights in resisting the seduction of self-absorption and that by benefiting others, we will achieve personal contentment. The Dalai Lama calls this "wise selfishness." Foolish selfishness is not concerned with other's welfare and thus perpetuates our discontent. Shantideva further warns that desires are endless and that there is nothing wrong with possessions -- the problem lies in our addiction to them.

I actually have no idea of my spiritual condition. I have to rely on personal barometers. I live in the upstairs apartment of a duplex. It is between 800 and 900 square feet of living space, and, it is perfect for me and my three-year-old Petite Goldendoodle dog named Fifi. The living room looks west over the St. Croix River and the sunsets are magnificent. I have three adult children and six grandchildren between the ages of 7 and 16. My oldest daughter Laura is my awesome co-author, Annie is the Rocky Mountain adventurer superintending a golf course and running a snowcat grooming ski runs in the winter. Paul and his wife, Julianne, are nurse managers and have a blended family. I attend weekly AA and Al-Anon meetings, sponsor four women, and have two sponsors. Most of my time is spent outside walking in state parks -- all year long. And I mow lawns, shovel snow, garden, and golf. I love my tribe of women, my children and their partners, and the grandchildren. That is my life today and I feel content and confident and healthy. I have no secrets, and, only occasionally, feel angry.

For the majority of my life, however, I became rageful if people and events did not comply with my directives. If I played a poor round of golf or had a bad sailboat race, I pouted for hours. Is competitiveness ego driven? I was paranoid and thought no one could like me. I trusted no one. I was intrusive in my children's affairs. I was a people pleaser and incapable of saying "no". I mentioned the lovely sunsets -- most of them I miss because I need lots of sleep and Fifi and I retire during daylight most of the year. And now I say "no" to evening events! I am learning "wise selfishness". We talk of HALT -- hunger, anger, loneliness and tiredness as triggers for relapse. Gratitude is the attitude and solution to all kinds of foolish selfishness, I think. Nutritious food, good sleep, and gratitude are signposts perhaps for a healthy spiritual condition -- an attitude of being of service to every living being we encounter. I can only hope that my words in writing this book are with an intent to help people, and not another ego trip. How will I ever know? -*Jane*

How do you think your spiritual condition is today?

"Serenity is always available to me, but it is my job to seek it where it can be found." *Courage to Change* p. 346

I will take responsibility for my well-being by paying attention to my physical body and when it signals stress.

I will be vigilant in observing my thoughts and how those thoughts create stressful signals in my body.

I will turn my will over to the care of a Higher Power.

I will turn my will over to the care of a Higher Power.

I will turn my will over to the care of a Higher Power. *-Laura*

How do you find serenity?

Pema Chödrön writes of an attitude shift: "Instead of just focusing on ourselves, we start thinking beyond "me" and "mine". Remembering the distress and hardships of others, and that enlightenment is possible for everyone, opens us to a bigger perspective." "Small gestures of love and concern can help heal the suffering of the world. The most significant step any one of us can make toward global peace is to soften what's rigid in our heart." Richard Rohr reminds us that: "Humans become like the God we worship. So it's important that our God is good and life-giving. That's why we desperately need a worldwide paradigm shift in Christian consciousness regarding how we perceive and relate to God. This shift has been subtly yet profoundly underway for some time, hiding in plain sight. In order to come together in politics and religion, to take seriously new scientific findings in biology and quantum physics, and for our species and our planet to even survive we must reclaim Relationship as the foundation and ground of everything."

I think my love of the natural world aided me to allow faith into my consciousness. This is a thumbnail of what I have learned. From nothing, a tiny speck of brilliant light appeared. It was almost infinitely hot. Inside this fireball was all of space. With the creation of space came the birth of time: the great cosmic clock began to tick some 14 billion years ago. In only three minutes, the lightweight particles were the survivors, and are still around today. Atoms -- the basic units that make up all the matter around us -- are built up of quarks and leptons. Delightfully named, there are six kinds of quarks (three pairs -- top and bottom, charm and strange, and down and up). The leptons are the tau, muon, and electron with their paired neutrinos. Four forces act on these particles: gravity is one trillion trillionth the force as the other three. The strong and weak forces are found only in the nucleus of the atom. The fourth force is the electromagnetic force. This Standard Model of the universe seems so simple but the more we know, the less we know. Why is gravity so weak? Why do these quanta/subatomic particles pop into and out of existence -- a place where space and time are non-existent (the quantum vacuum). How can a particle also behave as a wave and so have the ability to be everywhere at once? Why is the speed of light (photons carry the electromagnetic force) a constant? Why does gravity warp space? I choose to believe in a Creator. All of these questions point me to a Creator that is beyond comprehension and immeasurable in elegance, beauty, simplicity and mystically mysterious. I understand that I will never begin to have comprehension of the Infinite Creator. Buddhists chant "All human beings are numberless. I vow to save them all." Buddhists believe in reincarnation until every being achieves Nirvana. I believe that Creation and all creatures will be resurrected and participate in Divine Relationship. There could not be heaven without puppies and colts. The mystery of this happening is no different for me than the elusiveness of understanding the above questions about our physical universe. All is Loving Evolution of Creation.

The story continues. Remember that these quanta particles create the visible universe while dark energy and dark mass compose the bulk of the universe and that dark energy is causing the universe to expand at an increasing acceleration. More mystery but on to what we know. Massive stars that explode are called supernovas and in the fury of the explosion the heavier elements are synthesized. There are 92 kinds of atoms, depending on the number of protons in their center.

Hydrogen has only one proton and makes up most the universe. Our solar system began around five billion years ago at the edge of the Milky Way, one of billions of galaxies. Our beautiful planet formed out of the debris of a supernova and was only 1 and ½ billion years old, when a complicated molecule made of five simple kinds of atoms duplicated itself. Voila -- life! And for another two billion years only bacteria ruled. Some formed a greenish substance and gave rise to plants. Fast forward through single-celled organisms to gradually more complex species and dinosaurs and ice ages and continents splitting and mountain ranges rising and falling to 65 million years ago when the first primates appeared. Hominins diverged from chimpanzees around 7 million years ago and at least 23 species have been found in our current fossil record. When our species Homo sapiens finally arrived on the scene 200,000 years ago, we shared the planet with three other species of the homo genera: Neanderthalensis, Heidelbergensis, and Floresiensis. It took sapiens 120,000 years to leave Africa and to go on to occupy every nook and cranny of the Earth. Again, I have no words for the astonishing fact that the first duplicating life molecule (DNA-deoxyribonucleic acid) has evolved so that I can contemplate my universe this morning drinking a cup of coffee and scratching Fifi's belly. One of my favorite memories is gazing at a star-filled sky wrapped in sleeping bags bonded to the ground of the northern rim of the Grand Canyon. That was a magnificent sight. These three simple mantras of the Big Book remind me that if my ego is humbled by realizing its extremely brief sojourn in time and space, just maybe I will allow my soul to seek Divine Relationship/Love. And when I die, my quanta particles that are the stuff of stars are re-born into other creatures. -*Jane*

Do you prefer one of these slogans from page 135 in the *Big Book* and how does it affect your life?

"Just for today I will exercise my soul in three ways: I will do somebody a good turn, and not get found out; if anybody knows of it, it will not count. I will do at least two things I don't want to do—just for exercise. I will not show anyone that my feelings are hurt; they may be hurt, but today I will not show it." *AL-ANON FAMILY GROUPS hope for families & friends of alcoholics* pamphlet

When I first started Al-Anon and read these words I could not fathom doing these things! It didn't make sense to me, but I was suffering and desperate so I trusted that it would lead me to a better place. I FORCED myself to do them! I also had to remember to read the exercises each day so that it would become less foreign to me. So embarrassing! Now I chuckle when I think of how "out of shape" my soul used to be. These exercises have become ingrained in my being after practicing them for so many months and now years. I still resist but when I feel my resistance I try to examine what is happening with my soul in an open and loving manner. Thank you Al-Anon for teaching me a better way! So grateful! *-Laura*

How do you exercise your soul? Are any of these exercises difficult for you to do or comprehend? Why?

"Today I'm going to pay close attention to what I tell myself. If necessary, I'll stop in mid-thought, start over, and replace negative illusions with positive truths. 'What we teach ourselves with our thoughts and attitudes is up to us.'"*Courage to Change* p. 105

This practice is life changing! I wish this was a class in school similar to physical education. Exercise the mind to strengthen the soul! One trick that has helped me overcome negative thoughts is whenever I start feeling down, I trace my thoughts back to the original belief. After years of practice I've noticed that the thought is almost always (if not always!) that I am not worthy. Now I laugh about how predictable and inaccurate those thoughts are. They also seem to happen if I am tired or stressed. *-Laura*

If you can notice your thoughts, what are you saying about yourself?

"Today I will 'Let It Begin with Me.' I do not have to accept unacceptable behavior; I can begin by refusing to accept it from myself. I can choose to behave courteously and with dignity. My freedom and independence do not depend on any acts of defiance or confrontation. They depend on my own attitudes and feelings. If I am always reacting, then I am never free." *Courage to Change* p. 267

What a profoundly joyous way to live! When I choose my behavior to be courteous and dignified, I always feel boundless. I am free from regrets and feel pride when contributing to the world in a positive way. *-Laura*

How can you "let it begin with" you?

"Since there is no 'arrival,' no magical day on which we suddenly achieve serenity and live on forever free from stress or strain, most of us eventually learn to be patient. We find that we can trust the process of recovery to move us ever forward, even if it sometimes feels as if we're moving backwards. We learn from each experience, and over time we build quite a storehouse of wisdom as a result. Pain may hurt as much as ever, but as time passes, we can put that pain in context so that suffering no longer dominates our whole life. We can separate ourselves from our pain, so that pain---as well as happiness and every other emotion---becomes merely another vehicle for growth."
How Al-Anon Works for Families & Friends of Alcoholics p. 103

Recently my dad died and I had no idea how painful it would be. Because of Al-Anon, I am more aware of myself and becoming more skilled with identifying what I am feeling. I am learning to accept the pain. What choice do I have? When I fight the feelings, it feels fruitless and unending. I often watch the grief arrive with curiosity and after allowing myself to experience it, I usually feel surprisingly better. I'm still not "over" his death, but I feel the joy of life even while I'm grieving.
-Laura

How does pain and suffering dominate your life?

"Just for today I will be unafraid. Especially I will not be afraid to enjoy what is beautiful, and to believe that as I give to the world, so the world will give to me." *AL-ANON FAMILY GROUPS hope for families & friends of alcoholics* pamphlet

I had to "act as if" for many years of reading and rereading this maxim. I didn't believe it was possible and I just selfishly wanted to feel better. I forced myself to keep reading it. I had to retrain my brain. Just like the promises of the *Big Book*, it is true that "as I give to the world, so the world will give to me." *-Laura*

How do you give to the world? How does the world give to you?

"Abandon yourself to God as you understand God. Admit your faults to Him and to your fellows. Clear away the wreckage of your past. Give freely of what you find and join us. We shall be with you in the Fellowship of the Spirit, and you will surely meet some of us as you trudge the Road of happy Destiny." *The Big Book of Alcoholics Anonymous* p. 164

The pioneers of AA learned this fact: the best way to stay out of the bottle is to help another drunk. They showed the world that they did not have to go on practicing their self-destructive behavior. By coming to the truth about themselves, living honestly with others, and growing spiritually by being of service to others, a real personality transformation can occur. And almost a century later, this message continues: real faith translates into action, not just good feelings. By working with others we recognize that we are not the center of the universe and we no longer focus solely on our own needs. We have come to believe that an awareness of a Power greater than ourselves is the essence of spiritual experience. Jesus of Nazareth gives us some ideas about Faith. He tells us to look at the birds in the air. They don't plant or harvest or store food in barns, but they are cared for by their "heavenly Father." Jesus goes on to say that we cannot add any time to our lives by worrying about it. He tells us not to be afraid and that it is peace that he will leave with us. Jesus reminds us that "with God all things are possible." He tells his followers He is giving a new commandment: To love each other. He also advises to forgive anyone that you have anything against. I believe that practicing faith, hope and love will put us on our happy Destiny Road and that the Fellowship of the Spirit means my participation in the Divine Relationship -- loving the goodness/divinity/grace in me and all others in creation. *-Jane*

How are you trudging the Road or happy Destiny or are you still trying to find your way to this destination?

"Willingness, honesty and open-mindedness are the essentials of recovery." *The Big Book of Alcoholics Anonymous* p. 568

The Buddhist teacher, Chögyam Trungpa gives us this simple, profound message: "We all have the inborn wisdom to create a wholesome, uplifted existence for ourselves and others." Wayne Dyer wrote: "A person who lives in a state of unity with the Source (I say Infinite Relationship or God) doesn't look any different from ordinary folks." Dyer calls these people connectors (I use the noun "mystics"). However, Connectors can be very different from the crowd. Connectors believe in synchronicity or that seemingly insignificant events are being orchestrated by the Source in perfect harmony. Connectors live in a state of appreciation and inclusiveness (knowing that all of us emanate from the same divine Source). Connectors smile and remind others that the world of spirit works in peace, love, harmony, kindness, and abundance. Connectors are not afraid of death, are exceptionally generous, often get labeled as aloof and distant because they don't gravitate toward small talk and gossip, and do not spend time watching violent TV shows or reading accounts of atrocities and war statistics. Connectors are extraordinarily creative, exceptionally kind and loving, and open to everything and all possibilities -- asking "What can I learn, and how can I grow from what I'm receiving?" The Dalai Lama wrote on Twitter today (May 19th, 2019): "If you restrain from wrongdoing, people will see you as a friend, and you'll be happy. When people are wealthy, and powerful, but dishonest, people don't like them, even if they don't show it to their faces. If you do good, when you are gone, you will be missed."

Also in Richard Rohr's daily meditation today, he began: "God for us, we call you Father. God alongside us, we call you Jesus. God within us, we call you Holy Spirit." Rohr goes on to claim that when the Spirit is alive in people, they wake up from their mechanical thinking and enter the realm of co-creative power. "Like Pinocchio, we move from wooden to real. We transform from hurt people hurting other people to wounded healers healing others. Not just as individuals but as shapers of history that keeps moving forward through the Spirit's power."

All forms of human worship contain three entities: a Deity, Scripture, and Loving/Supportive Community. Christian, Muslim, Buddhist, Judaism, Hindu or 12-step program have the same Reality -- it is like pointing at the moon from positions hundreds of miles apart. Same moon, just different pointers. All hopes of experiencing heaven, enlightenment, serenity, and happy spirituality require willingness, honesty and open-mindedness. *-Jane*

What do each of these so-called essentials of recovery mean to you?

www.ingramcontent.com/pod-product-compliance
Lightning Source LLC
Chambersburg PA
CBHW040256100426
42811CB00011B/1278